This book belongs to

....

This edition published by Parragon Books Ltd in 2017
and distributed by

Parragon Inc.
440 Park Avenue South, 13th Floor
New York, NY 10016
www.parragon.com

This book is based on the TV series *Peppa Pig*.
Peppa Pig is created by Neville Astley and Mark Baker.
© ABD Ltd/Ent. One UK Ltd 2003.
www.peppapig.com

ISBN: 978-1-4748-5155-8

Printed in China

Peppa Pig ™

All About Me

PaRragon

Bath • New York • Cologne • Melbourne • Delhi
Hong Kong • Shenzhen • Singapore

Hello, Peppa!

Peppa is four years old. She is mischievous, and can be a little bit bossy! Her favorite thing is jumping in muddy puddles.

Color in this picture of muddy Peppa.

Now it's your turn to tell Peppa all about YOU!

How old are you?

I am .... years old.

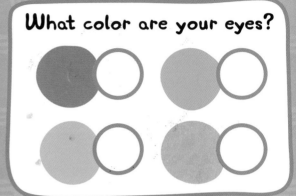

What color is your hair?

What color are your eyes?

Draw a picture or paste a photo of yourself here.

Hello, George!

George is Peppa's two-year-old little brother. He loves to play with Peppa, and his favorite toy is his dinosaur. Grrr!

Color in this picture of George and Mr. Dinosaur.

Do you have any brothers or sisters?
If you do, draw a picture or paste a photo of them here.
If you don't, draw a picture of your favorite toy instead!

Hello, Mommy!

Peppa and George's mommy is very smart.
She works from home on her computer
and is good at reading maps.

Color in this
picture of
Mummy Pig.

Draw a picture or paste a photo of your mommy here.

Circle the words that make you think of your mommy.

Happy   Grumpy   Smart

Funny   Kind   Cuddly

Hello, Daddy!

Daddy Pig laughs a lot and loves to play with Peppa and George. He sometimes loses his glasses, and this makes him grumpy.

Color in this picture of Daddy Pig.

Draw a picture or paste a photo of your daddy here.

Circle the words that make you think of your daddy.

Smart   Funny   Happy

Grumpy   Cuddly   Kind

It's Granny and Grandpa!

Peppa and George love spending time with their grandparents! Granny Pig cooks yummy treats and Grandpa Pig loves sailing on his boat.

Color in this picture of Granny Pig and Grandpa Pig.

Do you have any grandparents?
If you do, draw a picture or paste a photo of them here.
If you don't, draw a big boat or your favorite
yummy treats instead!

The Pig Family Tree

This tree shows everyone in the Pig family.

Who is above Peppa?

Which two pigs are at the top of the tree?

Point to the Pig family pets, Polly Parrot and Goldie Goldfish.

Can you create your own family tree? Paste photos of your family and pets here, and then write your family name.

The .... family tree.

Home Sweet Home

This house is where the Pig family lives. It has a yellow front door and sits on top of a hill.

Point to Peppa.

Is it rainy or sunny in the picture?

How many windows can you count?

Tell Peppa all about your home!

My home is in:

◯ The country   ◯ The city

My home is:

◯ An apartment   ◯ A house

Color this door the same color as your front door.

Draw a picture or paste a photo of your home here.

Peppa's Room

Peppa shares a bedroom with George.
They sleep in bunk beds.
Peppa sleeps in the top bunk!

Now describe your bedroom for Peppa.

I share my room:

◯ Yes ◯ No

I sleep in a bunk bed:

◯ Yes ◯ No

Draw a picture or paste a photo of your bedroom here.

Pet Pals

The Pig family has two pets—Goldie Goldfish and Polly Parrot. They are part of the family!

Which pet can talk?

Which pet has feathers?

Which pet lives in a bowl?

Use the colored dots as a guide to color in Goldie and Polly.

Do you have any pets? If you do, draw
a picture or paste a photo of them here.
If you don't, draw your dream pet instead!

Pet's name: ....

Type of animal: ....

Outdoor Fun

Peppa and George love to visit Granny Pig and
Grandpa Pig's house because they have a backyard to
play in. Granny keeps chickens in the yard. Cluck, cluck!

How many
chickens can
you count?

Can you
spot a
rooster?

Who is
wearing
a hat?

Talk about where you like to play outdoors!

I have a backyard:

⃝ Yes

⃝ No

I keep animals in my backyard:

⃝ Yes, I keep ....

⃝ No

I would most like to play:

⃝ In the forest

⃝ At the beach

⃝ In the mountains

⃝ In the fields

⃝ On the water

⃝ At the park

Dream House

Peppa and George love their tree house,
which is also in Granny Pig and
Grandpa Pig's backyard.
It's the perfect place to play!

How do Peppa
and George
get up to the
tree house?

What
color is
the door?

What has
Peppa used
as a flag?

If you had a playhouse, what would it be like?

A circus tent

A rocket

A hot-air balloon

A castle

A cave

A pirate ship

Peppa's Playgroup

Peppa and George love going to playgroup.
They paint pictures, play instruments, and shoot hoops.
Their teacher is Madame Gazelle, and she is lots of fun.

Point to
the globe.

How many
children are
in class?

What
has Peppa
painted?

Peppa loves art class. Draw around your hand,
and then draw a funny face and add color.

Give your funny friend a name!

My friend is named: ....

Best Friends

Peppa has lots of friends, but her best friend is Suzy Sheep. Suzy likes pretending she's a nurse, helping her patients feel better.

Color in this picture of Peppa and Suzy.

Tell Peppa and Suzy all about your best friend.

What is their name?

....

How old are they?

.... years old.

Circle the things you like best about them. They are:

Smart   Messy   Kind

Loud   Happy   Funny

Draw a picture or paste a photo of your best friend here.

Lots of Friends

Suzy and Peppa have lots of friends.
They all play together and have so much fun!

Color in this picture of
Peppa and her friends.

Pedro Pony

George

Peppa

Suzy Sheep

Emily Elephant

Rebecca Rabbit

Danny Dog

Freddy Fox

Candy Cat

Zoe Zebra

Wendy Wolf

Draw a picture or paste a photo of your friends here.

Pals' Playtime

Peppa and her friends love being on the playground.
They fly down the slide and spin around on the merry-go-round.

What would you like to go on?

Point to Peppa.

Which two friends are on the seesaw?

What is your favorite part of the playground?

The swing

The seesaw

The merry-go-round

The slide

The jungle gym

Vacation Time!

The Pig family loves to go on vacation.
They have visited cities, mountains, and beaches.

Where do you think Peppa and her family should go on vacation this time?

A sunny cottage

A snowy lodge

A big castle

Imagine you are on vacation and want to send
a postcard to your best friend.

Draw a
picture
on the
postcard.

Love from

Write
your name
on the
postcard.

....

....

What gift would you like for your next birthday?
Draw it inside the box.

Peppa's Hobbies

Peppa has lots of hobbies. She likes to bake cookies, dress up, hula-hoop, paint pictures, play instruments, and so much more!

What is Peppa dressed up as?

What color is Peppa's hoop?

What instrument is Peppa playing?

Do you have any hobbies?

Reading

Dressing up

Gardening

Singing and dancing

Playing an instrument

Cooking and baking

Playing sports

Watching TV

Drawing and painting

Playing computer games

Good Night, Little Piggies!

Every night before bed, Daddy Pig reads a bedtime story to Peppa and George. They love to hear about the adventures of the red monkey!

Which monkey picture can you see in the book?

What is your favorite bedtime story?
Draw a fun picture on this book cover.